MW00366458

Forever Grateful To You:

Made in the USA
Middletown, DE
28 May 2021

40588371R00066